DISC
DOGS

BY ALICIA Z. KLEPEIS

CANINE
ATHLETES

SportsZone

An Imprint of Abdo Publishing
abdobooks.com

abdobooks.com

Published by Abdo Publishing, a division of ABDO, PO Box 398166, Minneapolis, Minnesota 55439. Copyright © 2019 by Abdo Consulting Group, Inc. International copyrights reserved in all countries. No part of this book may be reproduced in any form without written permission from the publisher. SportsZone™ is a trademark and logo of Abdo Publishing.

Printed in the United States of America, North Mankato, Minnesota
092018
012019

THIS BOOK CONTAINS
RECYCLED MATERIALS

Cover Photo: Utekhina Anna/Shutterstock Images
Interior Photos: Gian Ehrenzeller/Keystone/AP Images, 5; Wayne Ramsay/Skyhoundz, 6, 14, 17, 21, 25, 27; iStockphoto, 9; Michele and Tom Grimm/Alamy, 11; Olga Ovcharenko/Shutterstock Images, 19 (top); Makarova Viktoria/Shutterstock Images, 19 (bottom); Matt Born/The Star-News/AP Images, 22

Editor: Marie Pearson
Series Designer: Craig Hinton

Library of Congress Control Number: 2018949079

Publisher's Cataloging-in-Publication Data

Names: Klepeis, Alicia Z., author.
Title: Disc dogs / by Alicia Z. Klepeis.
Description: Minneapolis, Minnesota : Abdo Publishing, 2019 | Series: Canine athletes | Includes online resources and index.
Identifiers: ISBN 9781532117374 (lib. bdg.) | ISBN 9781641855945 (pbk) | ISBN 9781532170232 (ebook)
Subjects: LCSH: Dog sports--Juvenile literature. | Flying discs (Game)--Juvenile literature. | Dogs--Behavior--Juvenile literature. | Games for dogs--Juvenile literature.
Classification: DDC 636.70887--dc23

Content consultant: Peter Bloeme, director of Skyhoundz Championships

TABLE OF
CONTENTS

CATCHING AIR

It's a sunny summer day in California. Hundreds of teams of disc dogs and their human handlers have gathered at a huge grassy field. Some dogs are having one more drink of water. Others are barking excitedly.

A young handler makes her way to a quiet spot in the corner of the field. She looks at her canine partner. They squeeze in a last quick practice session. After a few jumps and tricks, she hears an announcement. It's time to clear the field. She pats her Border collie on the head. They make their way to the sideline.

Disc dog is a fun sport for both competitors and the audience.

Disc dog Torch, handled by Kirby McIlveen, makes huge leaps in the air.

Dozens of dogs perform before it's this team's turn to participate in the freestyle competition. One handler does a somersault as part of her routine. Another has his dog jump on his back then launch off to catch a disc midair. Even though many teams have stunning routines, the young handler feels confident. She and her dog have been training for this competition for months.

After what seems like forever, the handler hears her name announced. She leads her dog onto the turf.

The music she has selected for her performance booms over the loudspeakers.

The handler and her canine partner twirl and glide across the field. She throws the disc to her dog again and again. Some of the throws are long. Others are high. The dog digs his claws into the soft grass, racing to catch a disc. At exactly the right moment, the dog uses his powerful back legs to spring into the air. The crowd gasps as this canine athlete spins 180 degrees in midair. He expertly snatches the disc and lands gracefully on the turf.

Before the choreographed routine ends, this amazing Border collie leaps onto his handler's raised knee before taking flight for one last catch of the disc. Spectators whistle and clap when the performance is over.

FLYING DOGS

Disc dog is a fun yet challenging sport. The canine athletes that participate in this sport are expert jumpers and catchers. Handlers compete on the field with their dogs. But the dogs are the true athletes.

Disc dogs make jumps that would intimidate many human athletes. They zoom across fields and leap high into the air. It's common to see them catch discs thrown more than 120 feet (35 m) away from them. They can leap 9 feet (2.7 m) into the air after a disc. Spectators of the sport are always amazed by the athleticism of the competitors.

AVOIDING INJURY

Disc dog can be a physically demanding sport. Handlers work to keep disc dogs safe and healthy. One way to prevent injury is to start by training a dog to do low jumps and simple tricks. This allows them to build muscle safely. As the dog gains strength and physically matures, it can take on higher jumps and more complicated tricks.

No matter the size, a top disc dog needs speed and good timing.

A HISTORY OF
DISC DOG

Today disc dog is a well-organized sport. But it began simply as a fun game between dog and owner. The date was August 5, 1974. It was game night at Dodger Stadium in Los Angeles, California. A college student named Alex Stein sneaked his dog Ashley Whippet into the stadium. Between innings, Stein and Ashley jumped the fence and ran onto the field to play.

Out in left field, Stein tossed a blue Frisbee disc into the air. Ashley leaped to catch the Frisbee between his teeth. Again and again, Stein and his high-flying pooch

Ashley had the ability to make spectacular catches.

mesmerized the crowd. After eight minutes, the athletic dog and master were forced to leave the field. Stein was arrested. But Ashley Whippet's amazing tricks caught the attention of many. After this event, Ashley and Stein received invitations to show off their skills at venues from the White House to the Super Bowl.

EARLY HISTORY OF THE SPORT

In 1974 the first noteworthy canine disc competition was held at California State University, Fullerton. This event was called the First Annual Fearless Fido Frisbee Fetching Fracas. More than 100 dogs entered the competition.

In 1975 Stein, Irv Lander, and Eldon McIntire organized the Frisbee Dog World Championships. Lander worked for the Wham-O company, which made Frisbee discs. McIntire was the proud owner of Australian shepherd disc dog Hyper Hank.

Stein and Ashley Whippet won the first three Frisbee Dog World Championships in 1975, 1976, and 1977. Over time this competition turned into a contest series with both Freestyle and Toss-and-Catch events. It became known in 1982 as the Ashley Whippet Invitational (AWI). Every year, teams that want to compete try out at events in the United States, Canada, Asia, and Europe.

THE SPORT TODAY

Disc dog competitions have become much more popular since their earliest days. Today disc dog competitions are held across the United States. Disc dogs also compete in many countries in North and South America, Europe, and Asia.

The Skyhoundz series includes more than 100 disc dog competitions around the world. Teams qualify to take part in the annual weeklong Hyperflite Skyhoundz World Canine Disc Championships. This is the world's most popular disc dog series. The classes in this series are the Skyhoundz Classic, DiscDogathon, and Xtreme Distance

KIRBY MCILVEEN AND TORCH

Kirby McIlveen was only 12 years old when she started competing in disc dog events. Her famous canine partner is Torch, a McNab shepherd. They won the Skyhoundz World Championship in 2011 and the Ashley Whippet Invitational in 2015 and 2017. Kirby continues to compete. She also teaches disc dog classes. Audiences and fellow competitors alike find the routines she and Torch perform together amazing.

Kids show off the fun tricks they've practiced with their dogs at disc dog competitions.

Championships. There are several other well-known disc dog competitions too. One is the Purina Pro Plan Incredible Dog Challenge. The US Disc Dog Nationals (USDDN) is another. Kids can also compete in disc dog events. Skyhoundz offers a Youth Division, which includes Freestyle and Distance/Accuracy, for kids under 16 years old.

DISC DOG CLUBS

Disc dog clubs began in the mid-1980s. But their popularity took off during the mid to late 1990s. These clubs are a great way to meet people interested in the sport. Disc Dogs in Southern California (D^{2}I.S.C.) is a successful club. It organizes clinics where people can share training ideas. It also plans informal play days, where members and prospective members can have fun with their dogs. D^{2}I.S.C. even holds its own competitions. People who don't want to compete can still join a club to gain skills and have fun. Club members often enjoy sharing their experiences with those new to the sport.

BREEDS AND
TRAINING

Many dogs can catch a disc. But some breeds are more common in disc dog competitions. Disc dogs tend to be medium sized. Dogs with long legs and long snouts are better suited to catching flying discs than toy breeds or snub-nosed dogs are. Long legs help a dog leap to grab discs. Lengthier snouts clamp down on discs effectively. But there are some disc dog competitions for smaller dogs. Dogs that measure less than 17 inches (43 cm) from the ground to their withers can compete in Skyhoundz MicroDog events.

Small or short breeds, including Pembroke Welsh corgis, compete in MicroDog events.

Disc dogs commonly fall into three categories. These are herding breeds, retrievers, and mutts. Herding dogs are often terrific disc dogs. Some very intelligent and athletic breeds are part of this group. Australian shepherds and Border collies are two examples. Both have loads of energy. They are intense when competing. Some experts say Border collies are the best-suited breed for disc dog. They are medium sized and athletic. Border collies want to please their owners. They are smart and very loyal. Some Border collies will catch discs for hours at a time.

Retrievers can also make good disc dogs. Both golden retrievers and Labrador retrievers are regular competitors. These dogs are medium to large dogs and muscular. Their instincts to retrieve lend them to successful disc play. These dogs enjoy training for disc competitions.

Mixed-breed dogs can also have many desirable qualities for disc dog. Mutts from animal shelters can be great disc dogs. Several World Canine Disc Champions were actually rescued from the pound.

COMMON
DISC DOG BREEDS

AUSTRALIAN SHEPHERD

Height: 18–23 inches
(46–58 cm)
Weight: 40–65 pounds
(20–29 kg)

BORDER COLLIE

Height: 18–22 inches
(46–56 cm)
Weight: 30–55 pounds
(14–25 kg)

Regardless of breed, all disc dogs need certain characteristics. They need to be energetic. They must be athletic. The best disc dogs are lean and flexible and have a strong jumping ability. They also must be intelligent. Disc dogs have to have a sharp mind to judge the flight of a disc and figure out when to catch it.

TRAINING DISC DOGS

Training disc dogs can be fun. It's also a lot of hard work. Before serious training begins, a veterinarian should check a dog to be sure it's in good health and ready for play.

Handlers should not encourage dogs younger than 18 months old to leap. The growth plates in a young dog's joints have not closed yet. Too much leaping too soon can cause permanent damage to those joints. Even so, handlers can still work with dogs under 18 months old. This is a good time for obedience training. Dogs are off

WHEN TO EAT

Disc dogs should not be overfed. This can cause them to become overweight, increasing the chance of injury. Meal timing is also important. Disc dog trainers typically suggest that dogs do not eat for 30 minutes to 2 hours before or after competitions, depending on the breed of dog. This helps prevent bloat, a deadly condition where the dog's stomach twists.

Whether training or competing, the most important thing is that dog and handler are having fun.

leash when disc dogging. Handlers need the dogs to come when called.

Before learning to catch discs, dogs should learn to fetch. Some call this activity disc groundwork. It can be done at any age. It doesn't matter what object the dog fetches. Some handlers start by tying a toy to a string. Then they encourage dogs to chase it. Handlers should act excited when the dog chases the toy. The most important thing for a disc dog to learn is to have fun.

Dogs learn how to catch discs at short distances before they catch discs thrown far away.

After chasing and fetching an object, the dog needs to drop that object on command. Once a dog can successfully fetch a toy, bring it back, and drop it, it's time to train with discs.

Disc dogs must be trained to perfect their skills of catching a disc in midair. Handlers often begin with very short tosses to their dogs. Once dogs can successfully catch these tosses, handlers will increase the distance of the throws. They'll also increase how high they toss the discs. Eventually the handlers will toss the discs just above the dog's head. The dog will then have to leap a bit in order to catch the discs. It's helpful for the handler to be good at throwing discs.

People can learn how to train disc dogs in many ways. One is by watching and learning from skilled handlers at competitions. Another is by watching videos or reading online articles about training. In areas where disc dog is popular, people also train with local disc dog club members.

DISC DOG RULES

Disc dog competitions include several different events. Judges score these events, and the dogs with the most points win. The Mini-Distance event goes by many different names: Toss and Fetch, Distance/Accuracy, and Toss and Catch. Most disc dog beginners try this event first. Handlers typically have 60 seconds to throw one disc as many times as they can. The dog retrieves the disc before the handler throws it again. The dog catches and retrieves as many times as it can during the allotted time. In this event, dogs are scored based on how many discs they catch and where on the field they catch them. A dog

In Freestyle, tricks that involve both dog and handler help build up points.

can earn additional points for catching discs when it is completely airborne.

Freestyle is another popular disc dog event. It involves acrobatic moves. Canine athletes might jump off or race around their handlers' bodies. They twist their bodies while up in the air. Freestyle routines allow five or more discs. They can range from 30 seconds to three minutes long. Handlers choose their own music. They also choreograph the routine. Judges give points for a team's athleticism and creativity. They evaluate the difficulty of various tricks. They also consider the handler's showmanship.

Besides regular freestyle, there's also Pairs Freestyle. This event involves two handlers rather than one. Both handlers work on a field at the same time with the same dog. They display complex skills. These include simultaneous throws and alternating disc throws to the dog. Pairs Freestyle also features other innovative moves. The scoring is similar to that used in Freestyle, but competitors can use twice as many discs.

Handlers get creative with their Pairs Freestyle routines.

DISC DOG SUPPLIES

Disc dog is a great, inexpensive sport. It doesn't require any fancy equipment. Participants need three things: a dog, a few discs, and some grass or a safe, open space for throwing. The discs used for this sport shouldn't be the plastic discs people toss to one another. Regular discs can crack easily when a dog catches them. The plastic edges can cut a dog's mouth. There are many types of discs made specifically for this sport. They are made from a special type of plastic that allows a dog's teeth to puncture it without cracking. Dog-safe discs have a rounded lip on their reinforced rims. This lets the dog bite safely when catching them.

RULES OF COMPETITION

Disc dog competitions have many rules. Some top competitions require a dog-handler team to qualify in order to participate. Teams can't just show up at the Skyhoundz finals. They must qualify at a special event. The top finishers at Skyhoundz Qualifiers receive invitations to compete at the World Championship.

Before a competition, handlers should make sure their dogs are up to date with their rabies vaccinations. Competitions may require dogs to be at least one year old or 18 months old to compete. Such rules reduce the risk of

EXTREME DISTANCE EVENTS

A more unusual disc dog event is long distance. In an extreme distance event, teams compete to throw discs as far as they can and catch them successfully. Male and female handlers compete separately. At the Hyperflite Skyhoundz Xtreme Distance event, teams have 90 seconds to make a throw and catch as far as possible. They repeatedly throw and catch during that time limit, and the longest completed catch gives them their final placement.

injury to younger dogs. Participants typically have to use specific brands or types of discs that have been approved by the organization involved.

Often, an announcer calls over a loudspeaker the names of the next teams to compete. The next handler then walks his or her dog to the field. The only people allowed on the field are the dog, handler, and contest officials. These officials include judges, timekeepers, and people who mark the location of a catch upon completion and make sure that both humans and dogs are in bounds during competition. Once on the field, handlers have to follow many rules. They must obey the time limits for their particular event. They must stay in bounds on the field. They cannot treat their dog cruelly.

Winners of disc dog competitions can earn many kinds of prizes. Trophies, plaques, and medals are common. Cash prizes are rare, but winning teams often get new discs. What more could a disc dog want, after all? Every disc dog event is both challenging and thrilling. Disc dogs are incredible athletes!

GLOSSARY

allotted
Given or assigned to someone, as for a task.

choreograph
To plan and practice each step of a routine.

fracas
A noisy quarrel or disturbance.

growth plates
Areas of growing tissues that cause the long bones in young people or animals to grow.

lean
Not carrying extra weight.

prospective
Likely to become something in the future.

qualify
To become eligible to participate in a competition after reaching a certain standard.

simultaneous
At the same time.

spectator
A person in the audience.

turf
Grass or an artificial grass substitute.

withers
The ridge between the shoulder bones.

MORE INFORMATION

ONLINE RESOURCES

Booklinks
NONFICTION NETWORK
FREE! ONLINE NONFICTION RESOURCES

To learn more about disc dogs, visit **abdobooklinks.com**. These links are routinely monitored and updated to provide the most current information available.

BOOKS

Bloeme, Peter and Jeff Perry. *Disc Dogs! The Complete Guide*. Roswell, GA: Hyperflite, 2008.

Furstinger, Nancy. *Herding Dogs*. Minneapolis, MN: Abdo Publishing, 2019.

Heeter, Melissa. *Champion Disc Dog! The Ultimate Guide to Getting Your Dog Airborne in 18 Days*. Kennebunkport, ME: Cider Mill Press, 2014.

Sundance, Kyra. *101 Dog Tricks, Kids Edition: Fun and Easy Activities, Games, and Crafts*. Beverly, MA: Quarry, 2014.

INDEX

ABOUT THE AUTHOR

Alicia Z. Klepeis began her career at the National Geographic Society. A former middle school teacher, she is the author of numerous children's books including *Trolls, Snakes Are Awesome, Haunted Cemeteries Around the World,* and *A Time for Change.* Alicia hopes to see a disc dog championship event in person one day.